WOMAN

A new beginning for you too

SHAMMAH HART

The Netherlands

This book is dedicated to God,

Who inspires me.

Blessed be the Lord!

It is a book to meditate on relationships and to remind us that the love of God is for everyone who seeks Him and call upon His Name.

Honor and praise the Lord and He will be there for you, forever.

CONTENT

PREFACE

I loved writing since my youth. I always had a word of consolation for others. Nowadays, I also write articles for 'Stichting Simia Literario'.

My inspiration to write is based on love and empowerment. I belief in the art of loving and to be loved.

I'm a life coach and the founder of House of Prayer and Miracle Ministry and the foundation Shammah Empowerment Global Health.

Dear reader, we can do nothing if the love for our fellow man does not prevail. Take notice that a leaf does not fall from the tree, if it is not God's will.

I thank the Lord Who is my hope and I thank my five children, for whom I live for their support. My thanks goes also to my sister Esther Jansen, Pastor Kayode Ifebajo (MFM Ministries), my dear friend Mrs. Ingemar Francisca, Assistant-Pastor Solange Pope, Steve Dundas, Prophetess Amarilies Marteszoon, my good friend Norwin Ricardo, who has translated this book and to all members of the House of Prayer and Miracle.

My prayer is that you will always trust in the Lord.

Soraima 'Shammah' Hart

WHY THIS BOOK

I wrote this book about 10 years ago but had it not published at that time. I decided to publish it now because I meet women and hear from them that they are struggling with the same things I had struggled with in the past. I want to encourage women, who just like me, have been thru difficult moments in their lives, to never give up. No matter what we go thru in live, we must not lose hope and trust in God.

When I think about the time which has been the start of the turnaround in my life, I see myself sitting with my feet on the sill at the house I was renting at 'Kruidenweg'. I stared at the sunset and suddenly the thought of what a divorce might lead to in someone's life came up. Pain, sorrow, hopelessness and all the debts you are left with.

My thoughts went back to the moments in which I contemplated to jump before a train and leave everyone behind. I remembered how the thoughts on my children would come up at such moments and made me realize again and again how much pain I had been thru when giving birth to them. What would follow was an impulse and drive to strive in life. Despite all, I had to persevere for my children's sake.

On that day I remembered how the thought on my mother, Mosa Jansen, would come up. My mother used to sing for me, over and over again: *"My child, a leaf does not fall from the tree, if it's not the will of God"*. The thoughts of my children and mother helped me to keep on fighting. They motivated me to not give up and not to live as a looser.

On that particular day I heard a divine voice from deep inside of me saying: *"I will never leave you alone. Come back to me and I will give you rest"*. These words gave me courage. I took a pen and paper, and wrote the words 'A new beginning'.

You can always start over. Despite all you have lost and all who abandoned you, you can start over. You may start step by step. Make a list and continue from there on. Do not sit down and let the days just pass by. Before you know it, a year may have passed by. Choose a milestone to achieve so you can have a new beginning.

I will discuss in this book, based on my own experiences, some topics which are of influence on our way of walking in life and certainly on our resolution to start over.

Love and peace be with you.

1. A NEW BEGINNING

The why of my new beginning

All what I had, what I have worked hard for to achieve, belonged to the past. Now is the time to explore how to make a new start.

When I thought about this, I was near the seashore at Almere-Stad, where many people were skating at that moment. My thoughts went back to my youth, at the time I was almost 8 years old. At that time, my life was so good, free and cheerful. I received all that I asked for from my parents. Our house was always crowded, because my mother loved to help people.

I also had a skateboard. We, brothers, sister and cousins, all went to the hill we called 'The hill of hell'. It was a short walk from our house. We had to skate from the top, via a long and narrow path, to the foot of the hill. If your feet were not steady on the ground, you would glide down to early. And understand me well, it was a steep hill, so…

Now and then we would avoid the trip, and we would walk downhill to where the schools were located. On the parking lot you could see all the boys and girls going around in circles or doing tricks with their skateboards. There was a lot of music, and everybody had his/her own skate style to exhibit. Those were lovely memories, I thought. My thoughts went on to the years that followed after these.

The years went by and the hormones changed us. The teenage years were fantastic, especially when a boy and a girl felt attracted to each other. We wanted not for our parents to stand in our way during this phase, because we were busy discovering love. We had no interest in good advice from our parents, because we wanted to experience what love is by ourselves.

When you saw someone, who made your heart beat faster than normal, you wanted to see that person every day. Gradually you approached that person until you asked him for his name. The smell of his breath was so pleasant, that you desired to kiss or to hug him. That person might become your partner, or the relationship might not go well, and all develops differently than what you had expected of love.

There on the shore at Almere-stad, I thought about all of this. My thoughts came back to the present and I realized that the years had gone by so fast. All I had been thru, both pain and joy, popped up into my mind.

I attempted to be strong and to hold in my tears, so no one could see them, but it was difficult. As a woman, it was heavy to bear all the responsibilities alone. The daily and weekly habits took me along, and I continued investing into them while I was still thinking about my pain and sorrow. I felt abandoned and alone. I had to get up for the children because they had to go to school. I woke up with sorrow at my side, and I wanted to speak to no one.

I accepted everything while wondering what my ex might be doing at that same moment. My heart would fall in pieces every time people told me: "*I saw your ex with someone. He looked splendid!*". A lot of my efforts went into thinking and I wondered: *why?* I thought maybe things would go better or there might be a chance for reconciliation and that he is coming back! I made efforts to think on something that no longer existed.

I sat there at the shore, lost in my thoughts and some tear drops found the way to my cheek. In my thoughts I was searching for a solution I had not thought of before. At that moment I realized that if I continued holding on to the memories, I would keep on turning on a roundabout. Up to that morning, had I been walking around with an imaginary heavy backpack and a heart full of pain.

That afternoon God made me realize that a woman does not give up easily. She keeps persevering till the end. That was for me the start of <u>my</u> new beginning.

Love, divorce and emotions

Pain and joy are the results of the decisions we make or have made. Often, decisions are taken too quickly, because of the bad aspects in us and our bad desires.

Proverbs 1 verse 8 and 9 states: *"My son, heed the discipline of your father, and do not abandon the teaching of your mother; they will be a garland to grace your head, a medal of honor for your neck"*.

Neglecting the advice from Proverbs 1:8 had consequences for many, also in their love life. Even today, people engage in relationships, despite the negative advice of parents and often the relationship does not work out. This happens with young couples and also with matured people. Every person has the right to choose whom to fall in love with nevertheless…..

There are people who even though they have (now) another partner in their life, they keep on thinking about their first love. Others are alone and think about their first love. They wonder why it had not gone well between them and their (youth) love.

Nobody wants to give up immediately on a relationship because things are not working out well. You put time and invests into it, so you can stay together, especially when you have children in that relationship. A divorce causes so much sorrow, but sometimes you see no other way out!

Consider some particular situations. There are relationships in which a child was conceived but the partner left. He gave up on the relationship and left the woman behind with the responsibility to raise up a child. There are cases where after some time there is a voluntarily communication between the estranged parent and the child. Some make efforts to contribute in the upbringing of their child. In other cases, although others are raising up their child, they keep having and showing interest in the child. Even in those circumstances it is hard because life had not gone as planned or hoped for.

LOVE IS SOMETHING

YOU CANNOT EXPLAIN.

TWO PEOPLE BECOME ONE.

LOVE IS SO DEEP,

IT IS THE SECRET OF YOUR FEELINGS.

It is human like to attempt shaking off the whole situation of a divorce from you. What do you do in such cases?

- Do you start drinking?
- Do you start wearing indecent clothing, and you are going to mix yourself in parties at bars and cafés?
- Do you really need to put everything on Facebook, so that everyone can follow your way of living?
- Is this a way of taking revenge?
- To show that you too know how to enjoy life abundantly?
- Is all of this really required?

Or do you choose to think, especially in the beginning, that nothing else matters and that you will not be able to achieve anything?

No sisters, quit thinking or acting like that!

We have more value than all that craziness in this world. It is true, you supported your ex all the way and you had great times together, despite the ups and downs. Nonetheless, he is **not** with you anymore. No, he is not dead. He is alive, but with another person. Now you are left alone with the children and you are instructing and teaching them all what the Lord commands. They look at their mother who is in a bad emotional situation. Come to Jesus, sister! He can raise your head up again for you to be a testimony for your children.

Don't delude yourselves: no one makes a fool of God! A person reaps what he sows. (emphasis added) (Galatians 6:7).

That's why I say to you woman: "***Stand up***. It is harvest time."

Woman, notice how heavily bend down you are because of your situation, with a mind full of the past occurrences. These burdens cause you, without realizing it, to walk stooping down. Your brain and muscles get tired and that leads to stress in your shoulders. You get headaches, because your muscles don't get the required supply of oxygen. It is evident that when you are occupied with so many things, you do not notice what you are dealing with. I say to you: "Stand up!"

My advice to you is to read the next Scripture, meditate on it and relate it to what is said above.

Lucas 13:10-13 *"Yeshua was teaching in one of the synagogues on* Shabbat. *11 A woman came up who had a spirit which had crippled her for eighteen years; she was bent double and unable to stand erect at all. 12 On seeing her, Yeshua called her and said to her, 'Lady, you have been set free from your weakness!' 13 He put his hands on her, and at once she stood upright and began to glorify God."*

We have looked at the way we feel and think in the early stages after a breakup. Life does not stop there. Life goes on and the question would be how you position yourself. Who are the people that you hang out with? What do you want to accomplish now? Do you want to continue smoking so you can blow out the pain?

The Lord has given us His only Son, so that all who believe in Him shall not perish but will have eternal life. What a pain we inflict to Jesus, who has suffered for us, when we do not separate from the evildoer; he who has only come to steal, to kill and to destroy. He steels your happiness, kills you by filling you with enormous hate and seducing you to smoke, just like a person without brains. The purpose of the enemy is to destroy you and to leave you behind without life (John 10:10). Do not allow the enemy to destroy you.

God has given the woman the gift to care for others. That is why the man has less interest in caring for others compared to the woman. We learn so much in life and yet we accuse a woman for decisions she had to take.

The fact is that a woman puts much hope and trust in her partner. If the relationship does not work out, she may get depressed and discouraged. Some stop taking care of themselves and let all things go weary. This way they become victims. There are people who must go to a crisis centrum, some get desperate and there are people who wrongly look for a solution in alcoholic drinks and different other ways that lead to destruction. They neglect everything and forget that they were not born together with the partner. They neglect themselves, forget their position, their potential and even who they are.

It is true that when a man loves and values a woman, you clearly notice that she begins to shine, and that peace is back in her life. God instructed for a man to take care of a woman, just like Jesus cares for His church. (Ephesians 5: 25, 26). Teach the men around you to love their (future) wife. Teach them to not to compare her with others and to value her like Jesus did with His church.

THE WIND BLOWS,

THE COMPASS SHOWS YOU THE WAY,

BUT LOVE, HOW DOES IT GO,

WHERE DOES IT LEAD TO?

We forget how many ways there are to receive help. There are different ways to help and to guarantee the fundamental rights of the woman, for example thru the organization 'Help Women'.

God listens to the heart of the woman, because He created the woman with so much love. That's why He shows so much tenderness to her. Sometimes we are afraid of people, or we are ashamed for their sake or our own sake, which leads us to indecisiveness.

Do not allow the situations to completely swallow your vision for life. Adjustments are needed, yes, but no abrupt end.

A new start in extreme situations

I worked for a while at the Salvation Army (Leger des Heils). I remember the stories of clients, men and women, which made me ponder and realize that one should only trust in the Lord, Who created heaven and earth.

There were several reasons why they could not take diligent care of themselves. As example, I want to mention the following two situations:

- Some have been on the street since their early age,
- Others were happily married, but things went wrong when they came home and realized that their wife and children had suddenly run away.

What would you have done in such circumstances? Would it have been easy for you to sustain yourself in such conditions? Wouldn't help or consolation be helpful?

Sometimes we talk about people who knock on the door of institutions like Salvation Army, without knowing what they have gone through.

Sometimes we talk about drug addicts, people with dementia or people who behave very strange on the street. We talk about them because we think we are the only ones having a sound mind, while we forget how much influence circumstances have on our thinking and behavior, so also on them. While working at Salvation Army, I noticed that there were businessmen staying there whom at some point in their life had everything well arranged. They were married, had a family but one way or another, one partner disappointed the other one. Due to that and partially because of debts they lost all they had, and consequently they lost the house too. Why didn't the family help them when such a situation came to pass? Sometimes no assistance is coming from that side because one partner married with a person, while the family was not happy about it. When the problem occurred, they were alone because there was no one who wanted to help them. These are merely examples, but they do happen.

Hard and painful moments in life can make you lose your head. Some must use strong medicine and there even clients who let themselves be used, in order to earn some money. I have seen how nervous addicted people become, when they could not get anything to smoke. I made efforts to tell them that God knows their heart. When I talked about God, they showed interest and became joyful.

After having talked to them, they all wanted to help me with my tasks. My boss was not happy with this, but I chose primarily to talk to people with need. I gave them the opportunity to talk so they could express themselves by recounting how bad things are and how much pain they have. I was there to listen and sometimes that is all someone needs. Listening to someone might be the start of a healing process and it gives them courage to strive for change in their situation, to strive to take action for the better.

We were born by the grace of God. Where we will be born, in which family or in which country it shall be, is not revealed to us at the beginning. Either you are poor or rich, black or white, it does not matter. There would be always something for you to do if you were not born lifeless. Get up, God give you strength, so you live. It is not for you to go and sit in a corner and moan. Change requires faith but also action.

What is next?

Do you remember the man in the Bible who was possessed? (Lucas 8:27). Jesus can deliver us from any situation we confront. What we should do is knock and call upon His name, because nothing is impossible for Him. God created us in His own image and resemblance and He is nearby. ***"Stand up, don't lose your mind".*** It is really difficult and painful, and yet you don't know why you are experiencing so many calamities. Despite that, don't stay in the roundabout where you are now. There is something better for you, because what you are going through now is not the only thing that there is in life.

You laughed when things went well between you and your darling. Now that the storm has reached your life and your darling has gone, you want to quit. It is hard and sad, but you must realize that despite all you have done together, you were born alone. People can get tired, the love for someone can cease, but sometimes we must try again and do the utmost to see what we can save of the relationship. But if you don't succeed, and he does not want to be with you, remember than that God is your strength. (Ecclesiastes 11: 4-10)

Despite all that you have gone through and notwithstanding all the pain you are bearing, put all negative thought aside. Think about what you want and look for alternatives. Brainstorm on how to proceed. It is important to realize that life does not stand still. (Romans 12:12). Keep persevering, no matter what you are going through.

Sometimes there are unexpected drawbacks in our lives. What can we do about it? Our heart keeps on beating, we are not dead. So, let us fight the fight and keep striving to achieve progress. It is true that in times of unexpected drawbacks you have the desire to just stay in bed and to let go off everything. You don't want to listen to anyone, not even to your own children. A time when you feel apathy after having gone through all that pain and all the time that had passed. Het is not going alright with you and you see no point in doing something. Above all of that, people come and tell you that your ex is looking good. Look at yourself: your face is full of stress. You feel old, miserable and do not knowing where to begin. And he? He has no responsibility. Undeniably, because he left; the children stayed with you, but he left. It is the time in which you ask God: *"What have I done wrong, Lord?"*

It is easy when someone comes and tells you; *"don't worry"*, because they are not the ones going through it. But then again, don't neglect your body! Do not deal with food in an irresponsible way!

Pain, yes, everyone deals with pain in his own way, but it is essential to not give up. Keep persevering, because your heart still calls upon the Lord for help. Do you feel so disappointed, that you don't even want to talk to the Lord? The Word of God says that we may approach Him from time to time with a sigh and without words. This means that with each strong sigh you release, the Lord already knows what you want to tell Him. (Romans 8:26, 27). In the same way, the Holy Spirit comes to help us in our weaknesses, because we don't know what to pray for nor how to pray. And the Lord Who examines our heart, knows what the Holy Spirit thinks, because the Holy Spirit acts according to the will of the Father.

Begin with a new start

Stand up, yes, stand up! Don't stay asleep and don't try to remember things that makes you cry. He is gone, it is true. After all those years he is not with you anymore. Now you must decide if you will remain alone or you think: *"you know God, send me another partner"*. You must stand up and put your trust in God, because He gives anyone who seeks Him a second chance.

Prepare yourself for your fresh start.

Look at yourself in the mirror and ask yourself the following questions:

1. While looking at your face, do you recognize who you are?
2. Is it you whom you see?
3. Do you see who is in the mirror?
4. Is it you?
5. Do you want to be like that?
6. Are you happy with what you are seeing?
7. Do you want to stay like that?

8. Are you happy with what you are seeing in the mirror?

9. Your smile, is it joyful?

10. Look at your body. Do you want to be like that?

11. What will you do with regards to your answers?

Go take a shower, wash your hair, dress up, wear a nice dress and walk a little outside. Walk around and don't think on things that will make you cry or sad. Try to make yourself look nice. Cook a delicious meal for you to enjoy together with your children. If you do not have children or they are not living with you anymore, realize that you are a valuable person and maybe also for another person who admires you in secret.

The Bible tells us something very important. That Jesus Christ creates a new person in us. Look up what the Bible says in 2 Corinthians 5:17. Someone who is one with Christ, is a new creation. What has happened is past, all is new now.

Come, you can stand up again!

Know that you are not alone. Know that you belong to God and that He guides and helps you. You can read in the next chapter how and what this implies for your daily life.

2. GOALS IN YOUR LIFE

Panic when directions changes?

I remember when we traveled to Paris with a family member. The map was our guide to our destination, but a specific location was not on the map. We got mixed up and we lost the way. We got nervous and started to ask the way, but the people could not speak English. We sought a gas station to inquire where to proceed. They gave us some directions, so we might be able to continue with our trip. We lost much fuel and time by trying to find out the way by ourselves. Asking for directions, helped.

You can always ask; you don't know everything, yet you should realize there is a goal.

When something goes wrong or your plan had not succeeded, do you ask yourself why you do get nervous, you lose your courage and you forget about your goal? Who knows your feelings, who knows what you are going through, better than yourself? (1 Corinthians 2:11). It is remarkable that when you are far away, you want to go home. You ask everywhere the way back home, but when you are in the storm of your life, you do not stand up to look for a way out. You lose our head and you do not think positively anymore. You lose your self-confidence, your courage and your lacking motivation for reaching your goal. Consciously or unconsciously, we act this way when it regards our love life.

You do not want to hear anything more about love, sometimes you beat your children or you jell to them, simply because the one you love broke you down and has inflicted pain on you. You forget yourself. But wait a minute, weren't you born alone? What's the matter?

I admit that I also experienced that situation. But, that day sitting at the shore at Almere-stad, I realized that the time had come for me to know what I want to achieve in life. I remember that on day, as I walked in the centrum, I realized that I should not hide myself or stay under the blanket. From that day on, I went out regularly for a walk and made efforts to look at my best.

A man approached me once and said to me: *"You are selfish"*. I asked why, and he said: *"Such a sweat girl and you are alone? Don't you know you are created by God to be around for others?"* I laughed and answered: *"You see my body? It is mine. God had not created us for us to be mistreated, but for us to be loved and cared for, provided we wait patiently"*. I had not realized how true and important those last words of mine were till the moment I wrote them down, and that brought up another memory.

I remember a client in my massage practice. She told me that she was not happy with her life. She had tried to be happy with many men in her life. When she said that I thought: *"People see you change partners often and they quickly think you are a prostitute, instead of thinking that you are seeking someone you can be happy with"*. Seeking so many companions, only because you do not want to be alone; just to have a man at your side. Is it true you want a man at your side just to have sex with? Why do you break up with a man and directly thereafter you have a new relationship with the first man who shows interest in you? As soon as you unite with someone, you become one. Try persistently to first know this man well and get to know his backgrounds.

Continuously changing of partner is a good example of not having patience and certainly an example of not waiting on the Lord. A constant change of partner is like riding a car and you got lost on your way. You become terrified and do not know where to go next. Do not lose your head due to the situation. If a relationship does not work out, do not panic but trust on the Lord Who created you. He says in His Word that the man will leave the home of his father and mother to unite with his wife. That is why woman, He has one for you too.

Love affairs, other relationships and yourself

We belong only to God, who has created us and has blown life in us. We have come into the natural world indeed by means of our parents, so we belong also to them. Who can take all of this away from us?

As an independent woman, who do you permit to rob you? Do you let your darling rob your heart or do you know how to handle with being in love and being dedicated to him? Fact is that you can love a person to the point of being crazy in love, but you must be always yourself. You don't have to let yourself go or chance completely. You are allowed to keep some independence, even when you love someone with all your heart.

Look at Proverbs 6:34. Jealousy can let the man get furious and makes him take revenge without having any regret. Therefore, never cause or provoke jealousy deliberately in someone else. Loving someone does not mean that because you are together, you are his slave. A love relationship is a two-way street. A boss-slave relationship is basically like a one-way road. A love relationship rather means to have company and strive together for progress in live.

And, if you do what the Bible says, you will surely achieve progress. Submit yourself to each other and have respect for each other because of the respect you have for Christ. (Ephesians 5:1-2)

It must be possible to be together and still have time for yourself. Time to think and to know what to do or how to act in life. You must have time for yourself, so you can take care of yourself. Besides, you must make time for your parents and your relationship with God.

In case your love life does not develop as you expected, do not give up and sit on the couch groaning. Focus on God and all that you already achieved. There is still enough to live for. There is a lot that belongs to you.

Name some things that belong to you. Below a start:

- ✓ My life belongs to me
- ✓ My heart belongs to me
- ✓ My feelings belong to me
- ✓ My face belongs to me

- ✓ My children belong to me
- ✓ My house is my possession
- ✓ My……………

We all know what belongs to us and what we have worked hard for. We also know what we received as a gift. God must always be on the first place, because without Him nothing can exist.

Set goals for your life

When you are living with your parents, you must obey them, till the moment you are independent and living on your own. There are children who say: *"Ah, I wish I can grow up quickly, so I can leave this house, because my parents are very annoying with their rules"*.

You want to move out from your parent's house, without knowing what you are going to face when you don't have the protection of your parents anymore.

Within that area of protection all is free; you eat, drink, take a shower and get new clothes. All of these are facilitated by your parents. There are also people who say that they will remain at their parental home, till they are married. It is splendid to stay at your parental home, when there is no abuse taking place. There are also parents who mistreat their children and that's why they want to leave the house.

You have learned everything from your parents, both the bad things and the good things. But, what do you want in life? What do you want to achieve when you are no longer under the wings of your parents? How are you going to take good decisions?

What you are right now, is that what you want, when you leave your parent's house? When you are an adult and you have not solved a problem correctly, are you in peace with your decision? Do you have a sweet darling? Are you compassionate towards others? Do you show kindness towards others? Are you a volunteer? Who are you?

In case your parents had not known how to express or show love to you, does it mean that you must act the same way? Because they neglected the law, you do too? To whom do you belong? Are you happy with your character? Your life, your heart, your time, all what you do, are you satisfied with them?

When we move out of the house of our parents, we breathe a sigh of relief: *"Oh, oh, free at last, no one to tell me what to do and keep disturbing me"*. Yet, when there are drawbacks and when problems arise, we still go back to them. We don't have to move in with them, but at least we want to hear their voices.

Despite what happens, let's realize that we are in a learning process and that we learn from each phase. When you move out from your parental home and you have not planned things out, your life will be like a puzzle. When you have a plan you cannot get lost, no matter how difficult the road becomes. Despite the obstacles you identify, you will continue looking forward. Your plan symbolizes your knowledge and what you have achieved.

Everybody cannot work on the garbage truck and not everyone can be a doctor. If there are no bakers, what would happen with us? When you go on vacation you need a map, so that you know how to get back to your hotel. When you want to achieve something, you need to know where you should or want to go. That's why it is good to think about what you want to achieve in life, before you take steps, and certainly do not act without reasoning. Put on paper what you want to achieve. This will help you to get to your treasure box. Now that the change has taken place in your life, it is important to adjust your goals and to start working on achieving them. Writing down the goals will help you to block negative thoughts and keep your focus on the goals.

Take time for yourself

Jesus Himself, the son of God, sought a moment to be alone so He could pray. He had not hidden himself, despite the many accusations against Him. He went back to the same people who were accusing Him. The question is, how do we behave on such occasions? Usually we would be discontent, think about what people told us, keep on crying and be displeased with and annoying towards everybody. We get sick and must visit a doctor, because of the stress. What can be done to make us feel happy? In these situations, the desire comes, to be accompanied by our parents. The point is that we must become independent, so we look now at the things which we can do by ourselves.

Notice how many things we are going through in life and yet, they cannot win from us. Even so, we allow our sweetheart inflict pain on us, with the consequence that we are not ourselves anymore. We must learn that we can give love to our partner, while still loving ourselves and achieving something for ourselves. If we are not able to love ourselves and care for ourselves, for our heart and to care for our feelings, how can we live happily and have peace?

Often time we fool ourselves. How is it possible to give all attention to our partner, acquaintances, friends, families, even children and all what is around us while on the inside we are not happy? When we breathe, we take in an air of despair. We cannot achieve change, if we have no strength to change ourselves. We must realize that we too can be happy, if we want it.

It is never too late to accomplish change, regardless of the years that have passed by. There is hope if we want to achieve it. If we want to see change, we should begin to think that our life belongs to us, our heart belongs to us, our looks, our time and our children belong to us. All around us belong to us. We will see change, when we realize that it has been enough with all that unnecessary suffering. God gave us Jesus, for Him to come to our help and to provide peace into our life.

Despite knowing all the above, it is not easy to let go of the past. You have a broken heart. It is an indescribable pain. A lot was promised to you, but none were fulfilled. It is true, it is painful to let go. Cry it out, shout it out, but be yourself. Tell yourself: *Indeed, he did this to me, but I won't give up. I will keep on going!*

It is painful, but don't let anyone mistreat you, because you are full of love and you forgive over and over again. Forgive and move forward. Be vigilant and always analyze if it is in your advantage, to have a certain person in your life. For this matter do not focus on financial or physical benefits but rather put attention to emotional and spiritual advantages.

A leaf falls from a tree, but after some time we will see another leaf sprouting on the same spot. Don't lose your heart, but allow yourself to grow again, because you are a valuable person. You are important.

<u>POEM</u>

Water as in the desert.

A path in the desert and I have no compass with me.

I don't know where I am heading to.

*It is like I am standing on sand not knowing how to
advance through the desert.*

We encounter this repeatedly on the love path.

*A leaf becomes green, then yellow, afterwards brown and
falls then from the tree.*

*Sooner or later, you will see leaves grow again and
flourishing.*

But in a relationship, how do you endure this?

*All the feelings you have for that person, how do you grow
again?*

Only the love of God can help us with everything.

You must entrust Him.

3. LONELINESS

Not only an unmarried person can feel himself lonely. A married person can be surrounded by many people but can still experience the feeling of loneliness. I remember how in my youth our house was full of people. While being part of that crowd, I felt lonely. Everybody would have fun when we had a party, me too! But, suddenly I would be overwhelmed by a need to cry. I would go to my bedroom and sit there for a while. Alone and all by myself. Sometimes I felt asleep and would miss the rest of the party.

I realized that when you do not focus on what occupies your mind, you do not understand it. Why, I asked myself too. Maybe because you feel you are nothing worth or that you do not belong to the group? Sometimes you must fight to belong to a group or to get to a position. No one is perfect, but there are cases we should pay some attention to. Each individual person must know what he feels. Your inner man, your emotions and your soul are seeking after something. God knows everyone. It is true, it feels sometimes as you have a heavy cross on your back which impede you to walk. Do not neglect the fact that Jesus had to bear His cross too. Nowadays we are enjoying the possibility to come before God, because of the heavy cross Jesus bore on His back. He took away all our sins.

There are people who join bad company or look for evil things to do. When you inform and dig to find the reason for those behaviors, you will soon conclude that it is only to fill the emptiness they feel inside. In such situations, you can talk to God and you will get the strength that you need. A pure and unblemished heavenly strength is better than an earthly strength that cannot help you. Sometimes these feelings can be so persistent that you feel like crying all along. You won't eat too. You worry about everything and don't want to speak with anybody, because you feel no one will or can help you. Sometimes people say that as a Christian you do not have to feel alone. If this is true, why had Jesus felt loneliness? The point is, Jesus had not kept on crying. He prayed to God. He sought the heavenly strength and this same strength can be found by mankind.

It is the human nature to experience or feel many emotions. Sometimes you get up and you just want to eat. Others want to get into a car and drive fast. Some others want to listen to music all day long. We may keep on filling the list. As I indicated before, who knows you better than yourself?

There are moments, sometimes when you are at a good friend or with family or at your job, on which your mind wanders, and you think: *why had I broken up with my ex?* On other moments you think about how many times you were insulted and mistreated without any reason. All these painful memories surface in your mind in time of loneliness. Despite the bad experiences, loneliness may drive you to contact that person for whom your heart still starts to beat fast. You call and then you hear: *"Why are you calling?"* The intonation and the reaction at the other end of the line causes that all the pain that you once felt, comes up again in your heart. Neglecting the pain, you answer that you just wanted to hear his voice.

How can that voice help you, when you know perfectly well, that there is nothing more for you there? It might sound harsh, but you must handle according to the <u>present</u> situation. Not that of yesterday.

We as women must value ourselves and figuratively not return to our own vomit (Proverbs 26:11). I have gone through this also, that's why I know what I am telling you about. Sometimes you waste money, by giving attention to an old relationship. Now you are without (pre-paid) balance on your phone and the question is, do you feel any better after the calls you made? Absolutely not!

I loved a person, indeed. I have put efforts into the relationship. Look at me now and look at him. He is all right now, he is the one who is laughing. Maybe he also has pain, yet he tries to let go of his pain, by acting the way he is acting now. A man does not speak easily about his problems. That is my experience. These aspects of life give us ways to look at ourselves and to get to know ourselves.

My advice to you is, do <u>not</u> ponder the complete day over your problems. You can get sick, by contemplating your problems the entire day. Maybe you want to call the person who left you, while you know how arrogantly he will speak to you. You incline to act this way, because you want to hear his voice and mainly because you feel lonely. It is better in this situation to scream it out and to talk about it with a friend, even better with God. You can gain new strengths out if this. Subsequently, go to sleep. A new day will bring the peace and joy you are looking for. Do not call him anymore. Forget all he had said to you.

There is no need for us to humiliate ourselves. Rather, we should know who we are and what we want. We should not allow loneliness to influence us to do stupidity when we are in this kind of situations. Remember who you are. Don't look for contacts that are not necessary. Realize that you are a precious stone.

What is discussed in this chapter are moments that you have experienced or will experience. Do not get mad at yourself. Accept that you must go through a process to get back up again.

There are women who decide to not have a partner again. They prefer to stay alone. This is possible but be sure to tighten your relationship with the Lord to avoid that you go throughout life with a feeling of disappointment.

Read and meditate on the following Scriptures:

Philippians 4:6-9
"Don't worry about anything; on the contrary, make your requests known to God by prayer and petition, with thanksgiving. [7] Then God's shalom, passing all understanding, will keep your hearts and minds safe in union with the Messiah Yeshua. [8] In conclusion, brothers, focus your thoughts on what is true, noble, righteous, pure, lovable or admirable, on some virtue or on something praiseworthy. [9] Keep doing what you have learned and received from me, what you have heard and seen me doing; then the God who gives shalom will be with you."

Psalms 29:11

May Adonai give strength to his people! May Adonai bless his people with shalom!

Romans 15:13

May God, the source of hope, fill you completely with joy and shalom as you continue trusting, so that by the power of the Ruach HaKodesh you may overflow with hope.

Psalms 34:14

[If you do,] keep your tongue from evil and your lips from deceiving talk;

Psalms 3

(0) A psalm of David, when he fled from Avshalom his son: 2 (1) Adonai, how many enemies I have! How countless are those attacking me; 3 (2) how countless those who say of me, "There is no salvation for him in God." (Selah) 4 (3) But you, Adonai, are a shield for me; you are my glory, you lift my head high. 5 (4) With my voice I call out to Adonai, and he

answers me from his holy hill. (Selah) [6 (5)] I lie down and sleep, then wake up again, because Adonai sustains me. [7 (6)] I am not afraid of the tens of thousands set against me on every side. [8 (7)] Rise up, Adonai! Save me, my God! For you slap all my enemies in the face, you smash the teeth of the wicked. [9 (8)] Victory comes from Adonai; may your blessing rest on your people. (Selah)

A prayer for the peace of God

Lord, let my soul be seen in Your presence.

At the moment of dedication to You.

Let Your eyes see me, Lord.

Let my steps, be very well seen by You.

When I call upon Your Name.

Please Lord, let me be in Your presence.

Because Your peace, Lord, is like a stream of clear water.

Compared with the nice morning breeze,

your peace lights up as the daylight,

like roses in a meadow.

Your peace, Lord.

I want to be like a tree,
which is planted beside a stream of water.

So that my roots can be fed.

I want to be there, where Your peace
can be reflected in me.

For my soul to get rest.

That Your peace and Your blessings in me Lord,
can be recognized by others.

Because You are my Lord, my everything,
and I will always rest in Your peace.

The peace of the Lord.

4. THE VALUE OF SINCERITY

A woman naturally needs a man to conceive a child. However:

- Who bears a child for nine months long in her inside?
- Who stays eternally with the responsibility?

The woman. The man can leave, but the woman is the person who always thinks, that she has a child with a certain man. The woman does not realize how strong she is, because she was always dependent on the opposite sex. Do not get me wrong here. God created the relationship between a man and a woman and determined the relationship of authority. The point I want to make here is, when things do not go well in a love relationship, how do you handle? Only a determined woman knows what she wants. She takes decision by herself, without worrying what other people might think about her. There are women who go thru these situations.

It is important to realize, that when a relationship comes to an end, you do not have to hurry to get involved with another person. Rather take time to think well about the why you think that you need another partner. Is it only to have someone beside you? If that is the reason, is it a wise one? There are women, despite having gone through annoying situations in their lives, who have not learned their lessons. When you had a relationship with a man who cheated on you or was addicted to alcohol or physically abused you or had not attempted to save the relationship, why do you have to accept these situations once again?

You do not have to hurry to get involved in a new relationship. You should make up your mind on what you want from another partner. Stop thinking that when the man treats you indifferently, that this is his way to show you love. Do not fool yourself. Love is sweet, pure and real. There are men who leave their house and see wrong examples on the street. You fall innocently into their traps and get physically abused. Everyone has his own story and problems. Some women leave their parent's house without truly thinking about what they want in life and become unexpectedly pregnant. Life can bring so many things along, but we can convey change, in order to be happy.

A relationship starts nice, there are lots of lovely words. He opens the door of the car for you to get you in, and you go shopping together. But, what happens when the relationship gets more serious? What happens when you feel that you are not as important as before? The other has turned distant, boring and there is no passion anymore?

Before continuing with what to do, below some examples of other situations that are common in relationships. There are also women who treat their man wrong and their relationship turns into a relationship filled with pain and distrust. There are men who take good care of their wives nonetheless the women misbehave. It might be that because of love and for not having to talk about the situation, that the men keep on persevering in the relationship. Unfortunately, some men do not speak out about their pain. Maybe they vent their pain thru anger on others. Perhaps thru physical abuse of their children or they try to heal their wounds on a wrong manner.

Often times we are not sincere with ourselves. Be sincere about your feelings. We must undergo regularly a complete cleaning, by means of analyzing what must be changed in us. A cleaning of our home is important. Simply let fresh air blow through it. Get rid of things you do not need anymore; do not store them. The same applies for our life and our emotions. We should know ourselves, clean up and throw away what is not good for us. A knock-out in your life does not mean you are dead, no!

There is always help available, for the one who indeed needs it and want it. If we seek the true heavenly strength, He will come and help us (Psalms 139). It is important to be happy with God. We know what we should do in difficult moments. We can knock (Matheus 7:7). Not everyone knows how to approach God directly. That is why there is always someone on earth who understands you. God made it that way, so we can help and motivate each other.

Let us look now at how to change the course of our lives. The Bible recounts how Peter fished the whole night on one side, without catching fish. Jesus told Peter to throw the net at the other side of the boot. Peter obeyed, and he caught a lot of fish. Sometimes we too should throw our net on the other side. It is hard and painful, but if we do not do this, we keep wasting valuable time.

How often do we try to do things and it does not materialize? What is it that we really want? In reality, righteousness will help us. Why don't we try to feel free within our feelings? The way we want our partner to treat us, so should we treat them. On the other hand, what should you do, if when you want to say something or try to explain something you get shouted at or there is dissatisfaction? Next a comparison for explanatory purposes. When you see smoke coming out of the hood of your car, you go off the road, turn the engine off and wait until it has cooled off. Once the engine has cooled down, you open the hood, to inspect and look at what actually happened; maybe you only need to unscrew the radiator cap to fill in water or to replenish the motor oil in the corresponding section. We could do something like that for our emotions and relationship. We could take a moment of silence instead of jelling to each other. There are several other options that can help to guide a relationship on the good track. Here follows another one. The couple could stay over at another place than home and take time to talk with each other. Due to the daily habits this happens barely or not enough leading to all undesirable consequences. The couple comes after a while to their regular environment with the determination to allow 'a fresh wind to blow' through the house and in their relationship.

Another option is to write. Look if you can write a letter, to explain what you feel and mean. If you want to share your life with this person, then you must guide the relation for it to go into another direction. Maybe you have tried a lot. Remember, you don't have to feel guilty, if you have done efforts to talk and to improve what had to be improved. Maybe it is the time for you both, to go with vacation. Sometimes it is good, to be alone. You get the chance to rethink on the relationship, allowing the flame to burn again when you come together. There is always a solution, if you still love your partner. Only God can give the wisdom to keep on going, no matter the situation you are going through.

There are women who married several times, searching for the one who matches with them. There are those who found happiness and there are others who are still searching. It is wise to trust God when searching for a partner. Indeed, God said in Genesis that it is not good for the man to be alone. This should not mean that we accept someone, merely for not to be alone.

It is very important to know the character of your partner. Never decide in a hurry, because feelings can change. You should know if it is real love. Woman, when you were alone, you were happy. Why do you have doubts now that you have a partner? The enemy comes to steal, to kill and to destroy, but if we call upon the name of Jesus Christ, He will help us in our weakness. Jesus said that He will be till the end of time with all who believe in Him. There is hope for you too.

A bird flies everywhere to find food for her young's. People will chase her, but she will keep on trying to achieve her goal. How more valuable are we? Woman, you are valuable; the man is valuable too. We are both important, so let's take care of our emotions and let He who created you, guide each part of your feelings. <u>You are not worthless.</u>

5. WHAT IS PERFECT?

People try continuously to discover better methods in this world. From new television or magnetron to new shoes. You will see now and then something new appearing on the market. It does not matter what is developed by a person or a company, according to some, there is always room for improvement. Simply said, humanity is always chasing after perfection.

The Creator of all is perfect. God said in Genesis, that all He had created, was good. In a relationship, you often hear one of the partners say: *"I have done my best to achieve this and that, but what will exist forever?"*

What God has promised, <u>that</u> will exist forever. Having people around you or when everyone leaves you, there is always one to whom you can anchor yourself and that is Jesus.

It is like the word of God says, there is a time for everything, but at each moment you must deal also with yourself. Today you are happy, tomorrow you don't want to talk with others. What is exactly good? You can fix or purchase all what is material, but your heart? Who can heal it for you?

You can love someone, give all to him and yet, he is not the one who will stay with you until the end of your days. When you met your partner, you were still young. With time you notice that he is changing. He is more serious and the person who you loved so much, it looks as if he is gone. When you met your partner, he took time to have a good appearance, but now it is like he has not even time to wipe off his forehead with a handkerchief. On a regular basis, we talk and judge others wrongly. Not only when a situation comes up but also while we were growing up and maturing. There is in every person something that you want to see changed. To some extent, we are all different which makes everything interesting and exciting. This is applicable for a love relationship but also for the relationship between a parent and child. We could say that we did all what was necessary for our children when they were young, and we still do. Now that they have grown up, notice their unthankful way of treating us. Let us not be preoccupied with this. There is so much else to experience. Above all, let us realize that God is our joy. If God does not give us joy, all other things are in vain. We can see a lot, we can compare all things, but only what God has created stays good, because He is the Creator of all.

A relationship gives you experience, and it makes you strong and wiser; you learn from it for all other types of relationships. There are people who prefer to stay in a relationship just to prevent causing (more)pain to others or themselves. They keep holding on, even if they go down. Some people are not predestinated to stay with the first person they have met in their life and there are others for whom it did work out well in their first love relationship. But, what is now perfect?

Either you grew old together or one dies early, there is always something new to experience. Partners in a relation, learn together what there is to be learned. How can you stay in a relationship which is dead? You feel only irritation towards your partner. The whole day shouting at each other, still you hold on to the relation, to prevent gossip and the pain which comes in your direction. How can you have joy and be happy with something, which no longer contains life? Are you thinking now, what should I do? Praying, that is what you should be doing. Yes, God is here, and He is never too late.

Before you take radical measures, deliberate if you can visit a relationship advisor. Talk, talk, and look for trustworthy people to whom you can talk. If after trying all of this, a relationship comes to an end, don't go sitting in a corner and think: *"Ah, I am alone now, I have no life anymore"*. God is and will be your strength.

For many years, I also cried and tried a lot. Despite all of this, my relationship of 19 years came to an end. There was physical abuse and pain. I had to take my decision, so I could safeguard my happiness. Before going for that drastic measure, my former partner and I undertook some steps together. There was someone we could talk to. This person helped us in the time that we were searching for ways to move our relationship back to the right track. There were a few more persons that we trusted, and we could talk to about our relationship problems.

These conversations made a difference, however, that was not enough for us. Please be aware that such conversations are merely meant as an aid. They are not the change that needs to take place in the persons, so the relationship can become a healthy one again. After all the attempts, I had to take a decision and I did so. What followed was pain and loneliness. Yes, loneliness, because I was alone. Loneliness after all those years of being together. Because of all I had been thru, I had to fight for not losing my faith in God.

What is de added value of staying together with someone I wanted not to be with anymore? It is better to take a decision to be happy and receive the peace of God than breaking up myself. I decided to end the relationship, which was choking me, even though we were both Christians. This confirms that even though you believe in God, that is no guarantee that you will not face setbacks in life. It is almost the contrary. Why? The enemy of our soul wants to destroy mainly those who believe in God. It is therefore important to invest in your relationship with God.

The process of divorce is exhausting; emotionally and physically. Many, including me, searched for support during those times. I had not searched for it in the right places or on the right way. The lovers, who came into my life during the hard times of divorce, led to nothing. It went on like that until I reached the point that I was able to say to God, that it was not His fault. Unknowingly, that idea had entered me. There were also some other thoughts in my mind. Thoughts like: *Why had God not prevented this? Why had He allowed this?* It took me time to realize that God wants only the best for me and all His children. Our own decisions and way of handling are the reasons for which God must allow things happen that do not have His preference.

God is good, and life is splendid according to our own perception, if we know what we want. I had time to think, while I had no other companion. I thought about my character and what I had to pay attention to in a new love relationship. I experienced how hard it is to be alone. A divorce may have an acute negative influence on the financial situation. That can have a reflection on your emotional status. It can go as far as you lose your job and there are no entities, who can or will help you.

While looking for help, you might lose your self-confidence and even forget who you are in Christ. I am pointing this out because of my own experience. In that period of my life, I was focused on staying alive and just live. Consequently, I lost my self-respect. During that time, I wanted to start my own business, but the pressure from others was so high that I had no space. I was not able to take time for making plans and start up the process the way it should be done. Additional adversities made me wish to travel far away. That idea of travelling as far as possible overwhelmed my mind, but how to make it possible? I tried to arise out of the pit on my own strengths and had no success. A turnaround came but a process was needed before it could happen.

There was no progress until I felt a calling from my inner man and my heart commanded me to go back. *"Go back to God!"* That was a cry from within me. I went to seek God again. After experiencing the peace that one can only feel when the presence of the Lord is present, I started to realize that I had to go on with my life. I was at that moment ready to think about questions like: *Am I ready to marry again? Am I ready to give account of my acts? Am I ready to lose my sleep for paying attention and sit and talk about how the day was? Am I ready to cook each day and to prepare his lunch for work? Or do I want only the advantages and not the disadvantages of a relationship?*

The answers to these questions reveal whether you are ready or not for a new relationship. You must wait until you have found yourself. Wait until you are satisfied with yourself and that you can take care of others. Nothing is impossible when you belief. If you have a dream or a plan, you can fulfill them if you believe. If your heart is still beating, it means you are alive. Don't quit on your dream or plan. Keep persevering, keep trying, until you see, what you always wanted to see, being accomplished (Isaiah 51).

The perfect relationship, the perfect partner and the perfect you. Do not worry if you realize that the word 'perfect' does not fit in the previous sentence. Only Jesus was and is perfect. As humans we have our limitations and less good aspects.

However, this does not mean, that we, together as a family or couple, cannot strive to build and maintain a good relationship. Sometimes, we fail to maintain the good relationship. Then choices must be made.

It is not the will of God that marriages end up in divorces. He wants us to be happy. As children of God, we should not think lightly about a divorce; absolutely not. However, it can happen that divorce is the only solution in a specific situation. So, make sure that it is also the very last option. Try all other possibilities first.

I had to make a choice at the time. I had gone through a lot without it being (completely) my fault. After having tried a lot, I had chosen for myself. In retrospect, it worked out well; both for me and for my ex. Today my ex is happy married. He continued serving God which is great. That is also a sign of the mercy and forgiveness of the Lord towards His children.

At the end, all worked out well for me too. Afterwards I realized that I am a pearl. Not just a pearl, but a special one in Gods' Hand. You are that too. Let go of perfection and focus on your relationship with God. He who is perfect, ensures that everything is alright in your life. I know He will do it for you, because He has done it for me.

6. DO SOMETHING ELSE

Genesis 1:15 recounts how God created mankind and gave him the paradise of Eden to live in. The man had to rule over all things. Nowadays, he must toil, to earn his every day's bread. They lived for a period in peace in the paradise, but because of their sin, they had to live differently than they were used to before. Getting used to a new way of living is something that we experience till date. A change in our lifestyle might be the consequence of moving, a family member that passed away, a new job or break up of a relationship. That is life. Just because something seems inevitable, doesn't mean that all is set. You should look into something (else) to do. We must realize that the end of something offers the possibility to start with something new. Something that maybe you haven't even thought of.

Let me tell you of my experience with the aforementioned. I remember an encounter with an acquaintance. Her name is Margaritha. I met her one day and she told me that her husband left her for another woman. She said to me: *"Now that he is gone, I am relieved. Now I have time for myself. I can do a lot which were not possible before"*. I asked her if she is now less busy in the kitchen as she used to be. She laughed and after giving me a big smile she said: *"We walk unnecessary with stress. The only thing we should do is talking to others and to tell them what our wishes are. Something different or another relationship. By communicating and share your feelings with others, you will understand each other. There is nothing better than to know that people are compassionate with you"*. Her answer was for me an indication that she no longer stressed out with regards to the diner. In fact, she is now aware of the possibilities she has for that task.

When something ends, we can learn a lot from what we have experienced. We become mature and more aware and able to make better decisions. When something ends, it has also its good side, because we learned our lesson from it.

Something different means, undertaking something that you do not do normally and above all, the encourage to do it.

Plan for instance a day to step into a bus and to go to a far place for some time. You can see and explore something different. You get the chance to rethink on what you want to do. Proverbs 17:22 says *"A happy heart is good medicine, but low spirits sap one's strength."* Therefore, my advice to you is, no matter how bad the situation, look at it from the positive side. That way you can activate the healing power of joy in you. Far more important than joy, is it to allow God to be part of your plans and even your thoughts. Proverbs 16:3 says: *"If you entrust all you do to Adonai, your plans will achieve success."*

Every moment in life counts. One moment is the only thing we have. What we decide, think and say in the now, is the basis for our handling in the future. If you want good results, think positive and don't go with the storm, which brings destruction. Take a moment to reflect on the aforementioned and think on what you can do.

Ecclesiastes 9:10 states *"Whatever task comes your way to do, do it with all your strength; because in Sh'ol, where you will go, there is neither working nor planning, neither knowledge nor wisdom."*

My friend Ingemar Francisca, pedagogue and stimulator of conflict resolution, said once to me: *"Shammah, we have to look at what is the best thing to do to improve the situation. We should accept that we don't have to feel ourselves ashamed, when someone offend us. I do not shout, and I don't want to be shouted to. I decide how I act"*. When she told me this for the first time, I thought: *"Indeed, she is right"*.

After reflecting on Ingemar's words, I decided to do things differently. I wanted to bring along change in my household and in myself. Why am I getting upset? Why am I worrying till the point that I get sick, while I could stay calm and explain myself? I have the time to stay calm, without getting abnormal heart beats. You might be thinking after having read this: hey, I can do that too! That is wonderful! Proverbs

15:1 says: *"A gentle response deflects fury, but a harsh word makes tempers rise"*.

I learned the following expression from Inge: *What can I do so I be better off?* This is a good question. *What can you do for things to go well at home?* We have as woman an important task at home. We are to comfort our children and our husband. Notice, what happens in a household when the mother is sick in bed and not able to get up. Everyone is upset, the household is turned upside down. The man and the children want nothing else than for the mother to heal quickly. This same way we must consider the Lord in our live. If we know God and we know His love, we shall not feel lifeless. We must be women who possess something different.

Jeremiah 33:3 states: *"Call out to me, and I will answer you - I will tell you great things, hidden things of which you are unaware."*

Jeremias 32 verse 40 says: *"I will make with them an everlasting covenant not to turn away from them, but to do them good; I will put fear of me in their hearts, so that they will not leave me."*

When someone talks about us, what shall they say about us? Good things or bad things? Would they say a nice person to talk to? Indeed, situations can lead us to be rude and insulting words may come out of our mouth, while we know very well that God warns in Ephesians 4:29 thru the words: *"Let no harmful language come from your mouth, ..."*. Don't use misplaced or offensive words. Talk wise and constructive words, while paying attention at the timing of using those. Constructive words can help those who listen to them.

We should stop talking about yesterday as if it is our present. There are moments that we should talk about yesterday, but only to let people know what we have gone through and show that despite all we have achieved something, and we can be happy. As a witness of what God can do for mankind, you encourage a person with your testimony, so she does not cling on to her present situation.

We read in Isaiah 43 verses 18 and 19*: "Stop dwelling on past events and brooding over times gone by; I am doing something new; it's springing up - can't you see it? I am making a road in the desert, rivers in the wasteland. And now says the Lord: 'Do not think what has happened yesterday, do not keep thinking of the past. Behold, I Am going to start something new, it is taking form, you can see it already: a way in the desert, rivers in the savannah'."*

Give your live another meaning and another color. You have the power to change your life, to change sickness into healing and the power to forgive someone who has inflicted pain on you. Forgive and let go; you can do that. You can change disdain into forgiveness and strive to upgrade yourself.

People are, better said you are, created in the likeness of God and you want to mistreat yourself? No! You are valuable. Think, communicate, meditate and take a moment for yourself to do something different. Do something nice. We were born alone. One thing we know for sure, when the time comes, we all pass away alone. Yes, we will die alone.

Concerning the life we are leading, each one lives it on its own way. You and I are still alive. What would you do or do differently? Do something positive!

We don't have to accept abuse and mistreatment. Do not accept a life of pain and sadness (Philippians 4:4). Put your joy in the Lord. I repeat, rejoice in the Lord! Do something different, look for something new, look for new contacts. One thing I have noticed is that, for example, when you go to a beauty salon, you will meet people you can listen to and talk to. In this way you connect with others and you talk about other things and not only about your pain. At church there are women meeting together and you will hear from women that have also gone through tough situations and how they have been victorious. Do not remain stuck, do something new, something different.

> REJOICE, REJOICE
> AND TRUST THAT GOD LOVES YOU
> AND THAT HE IS YOUR POWER.
> HE WILL NEVER FAIL YOU.

7. PRAY

Now is time for change. Now is the time to say: *'it's enough!'*. Stand up and dare to fight. It is never late if you truly want change. It is not late to declare and to put in practice, what you want to see realized in your life.

Bishop Bernard from the 'OAB Ministry Worldwide and Family' says: *"There is nothing higher than God and there is nothing lower than hell. Things might not work out as you want, but you can decide to do what you want to do"*.

You should not continue talking about what you have gone through, otherwise you are going to feel tired and without hope.

You shouldn't let the situation decide your future for you. You must take back what the enemy robbed from you.

- Take back your joy!
- Take back your peace!
- Take back your love!
- Take back your intelligence!
- Take back your wishes!
- Take back ………..
- Take back ………..

You may ask yourself how you will achieve the abovementioned. In some way my sister, it is easier than you think. You can take back everything that the enemy has stolen from you by praying. Yes, PRAY! A woman who prays, breaks down all negative thoughts. A woman who prays and trusts in God, should realize that she is battling against the enemy being the devil and his followers. Fight and call upon the name of Jesus, in order to win from the enemy. Call upon the name of Jesus to overcome bitterness, sadness, loneliness, revenge and spiritual imprisonment.

Ephesians 6:10-19 tells us *[10] Finally, grow powerful in union with the Lord, in union with his mighty strength! [11] Use all the armor and weaponry that God provides, so that you will be able to stand against the deceptive tactics of the Adversary. [12] For we are not struggling against human beings, but against the rulers, authorities and cosmic powers governing this darkness, against the spiritual forces of evil in the heavenly realm. [13] So take up every piece of war equipment God provides; so that when the evil day comes, you will be able to resist; and when the battle is won, you will still be standing. [14] Therefore, stand! Have the belt of truth buckled around your waist,[b] put on righteousness for a breastplate,[c] [15] and wear on your feet the readiness that comes from the Good News of shalom.[d] [16] Always carry the shield of trust, with which you will be able to extinguish all the flaming arrows of the Evil One. [17] And take the helmet of deliverance;[e] along with the sword given by the Spirit, that is, the Word of God; [18] as you pray at all times, with all kinds of prayers and requests, in the Spirit, vigilantly and persistently, for all God's people. [19] And pray for me, too, that whenever I open my mouth, the words will be given to me to be bold in making known the secret of the Good News."*

IT IS ENOUGH WITH THE PAINFUL

SITUATION, WHICH I WENT

THROUGH YESTERDAY.

My sisters, seek your strength in the Lord. Put on the whole armor that God gave you, so you can fight by means of the great strength that God has given you against the devil and his deceitful plans. Know that your battle is not against people, but against the leaders and authorities of the dark world and against the evil ghosts, who live in the dark regions of heaven.

Pray for protection against evil, that pursuit people, to take him/her in his possession and to destroy him.

Pray for our children, for our husband, for our houses, for our properties and for our possessions.

Pray against the malicious, invincible and dark supernatural powers. Jesus is the only mediator between people and God. That's why in His name we declare our freedom and deliverance (1 Timothy 2:5).

A few examples of effective intercession and prayer in the Bible are:

- Samson talked to God and God gave him power again (Judges 16:28). Samson supplicated the Lord: "*Adonai Elohim, just this once, please, think of me, and please, give me strength, so that I can take revenge on the P'lishtim for at least one of my two eyes*".
- Debora prayed, went to battle and won (Judges 4).
- Peter prayed and the man who was crippled, stood up and walked (Acts 3).

There exists only one God and one mediator between God and mankind and that is Jesus Christ. In the century where we are now, we should pray more frequently. We are approaching more and more the words stated in the Bible: *"Be prepared, because My arrival is near"*.

The signs of this are becoming clearer and clearer. Look around you and at the world. The days are passing by more rapidly, there are more wars, more accidents with airplanes, more earthquakes, etc. Let us turn or return to God, my brothers and sisters. Let us not beat too much around and let us seek God. Go to the house of God to listen to what His will is and to praise Him together with your brothers and sisters.

Maybe our (grant)parents had not to pray and search God as much as us now. why? Because our (great)grandparents were faithful to God. They obeyed the commandments of God. Today we want to do a lot ourselves and we forget what we were taught by our ancestors. Therefore, let us from now on put again our faith in God. James 5:13 says, *"Is someone among you in trouble? He should pray. Is someone feeling good? He should sing songs of praise"*.

Proverbs 31 talks about an exemplary woman who cares for her family every day, starting from the early hours. She wakes up to look for ways on how to go thru the day in abundance. This is certainly an example that we should follow nowadays. Don't you think that this woman invested in her relationship with God? Having a relationship with God means more than praying alone though praying is a good starting point.

You have no idea what to pray for? Below a brief list to help you out.

1. Pray for your children.
2. Pray for change in your situation.
3. Pray for your husband, even your ex.
4. Pray for your family.
5. Pray and lead a life dedicated to God.
6. Pray for not living a live like pagans.

OUR SINS ARE FORGIVEN.

PRAY FOR THE WISHES IN YOUR LIFE.

PRAY WITHOUT DOUBTING.

Some say: we know God, so we pray at home. Let's change that slightly and start talking to God. A prayer must not always be a solemn occasion. A prayer can also be in the form of having a conversation with God. Tell Him how and what you feel. Ask Him questions and allow Him to answer you thru His Word.

The Father tells us sometimes, up to now, you have not asked anything in My name. The Word says: *"Ask and your joy will be complete"*. By faith and if we believe what we say, it will be accomplished, by God who is in heaven.
(Hebrews 11)

"In fact, whatever you ask for in my name, I will do; so that the Father may be glorified in the Son. 14 If you ask me for something in my name, I will do it." (John 4:13,14) Read also John 16:14 and Romans 3:25-26.

Pray and ask the Father to support you in your search for a new beginning. Pray and ask the Father to be with you for the rest of your life and to provide you with protection, advice and if needed consolation.

A NEW BEGINNING,

STARTING FROM

PRAYER AND FAITH,

FOR YOU TOO.

APPENDIX PRAYER POINTS

In this section you will find some prayer points that I have compiled to support you when you are praying. This list is not limitative. As you go on praying, feel free to broaden or complement them. Remember, pray from your heart, God shall answer your prayer.

1. All what I have done in my life, conscious or unconscious, contrary to Gods Words, I ban them out of my life and I ask YOU for forgiveness, in the name of Jesus.

2. All what prevents me to progress, I break and destroy them in the name of Jesus.

3. All the wicked spirits who do evil, so that I cannot progress, I break your power and I bind you according to Matthew 18:18 in the name of Jesus.

4. All wicked spirits that attack my family, so that generations will undergo the same circumstances, by creating a fixed pattern, today I command you in the name of Jesus to release me and my generations. Let us go in the name of Jesus.

5. All evil powers who attack my children, with the consequence that they become disobedient. Today you let go of my children, in the name of Jesus. They will obey God and me!

6. All altars, which were made by my (grand)parents to give offers to false gods, I destroy them in the name of Jesus.

7. All doors which prevent me from achieving my goals are closed in Jesus name. The doors which lead me to a better life, be opened in Jesus name. I command: Closed doors, open as soon as I call your name. Closed door of ….. (*name it*), open for me, open in the name of Jesus.

8. What is coming in my direction and prevents me to have a job, to have a house, to have a healthy financial situation, …. (*name them*). These evil ghosts that come to sour the lives of people are the cause of my bad financial situation. Today in the name of Jesus, I command you to

release me. I proclaim freedom in my financial situation, in the name of Jesus.

9. Sickness, … (*name the sickness which is tormenting you*). Today in the name of Jesus, I ask you Lord God to heal me. I declare that I am healed. I am healed in the name of Jesus.

Pray for what you want to happen in your life. Name them and declare them in the name of Jesus, amen. Belief in what you are asking. Without faith it is impossible for people to see God move in their lives. God is love and all who stays in Him, are called the sons of God. (1 John).

Rejoice always,
pray without ceasing,
give thanks in all circumstances;
for this is the will of God
in Christ Jesus for you.
1 Thessalonians 5:16-18 (ESV)

ABOUT THE AUTHOR

Soraima 'Shammah' Hart is a brave and talented woman. She was born in Willemstad Curaçao (formerly the Netherlands Antilles). She grew up in the neighborhood of Jongbloed. She met Jesus Christ in 1990 and serves God in the Netherlands as a Pastor of the Church House of Prayer and Miracle. She is the president of the foundation Shammah Empowerment Global Health.

She attended the courses 'Science of humanity' at the Open University in Amsterdam and 'Pastoral Counsel' and 'Life coaching psychology' in Nieuwegein. Shammah is massage therapist, author, poetess, worshipper and life coacher. She lives together with her five children in the Netherlands.

For contact with Shammah: shaempowert@hotmail.com

www.ingramcontent.com/pod-product-compliance
Lightning Source LLC
Chambersburg PA
CBHW020737160726
47993CB00006B/2494